BATTLE OF GETTYSBURG

A History from Beginning to End

Table of Contents

Introduction

You can't tell the story of a battle without first telling the story of the war. But a conflict like the Civil War can't be broken down into a handful of sentences.

The simple explanation that we're given in grade school doesn't suffice. People didn't just wake up one day and say, "Let's have a war"; nor were there simple answers or simple causes. It was more than a war over slavery, or a fight to reunify a country torn asunder, though both became important factors in the conflict.

Whether about the rights of the states, or slavery, or taxation, whether nationalism played a part (it did and would throughout the war), the facts remain the same. Things came to an ugly head when the Southern states seceded from the United States beginning in December of 1860 that began in a single shot, the first, fired at Fort Sumter on April 12, 1861. For better or for worse, the country was at war with itself, a horrifying ordeal that wouldn't end until May 9, 1865, with more than half a million soldiers dead – 2.5% of the entire country's population – and what's estimated to be more than a billion dollars' worth of destruction.

The Battle of Gettysburg came about halfway through – a three-day massacre that became known as the bloodiest battle of the Civil War. Were 45,000 to 52,000 casualties worth it? I'll leave that for you to decide. But what was later called "The High Water Mark of the Rebellion" had an impact that can't be denied.

Let's see how it all happened.

Chapter One

Before July there was Lee

"The Trouble with Hooker is that he's got his headquarters where his hindquarters ought to be."

—Abraham Lincoln

Every good drama requires first a cast. The players in this particular scenario were men, rather flawed sometimes, some with little to no experience at war, though more than one rose to the occasion. People were sometimes petty. They played politics and worried about their own careers. And they made decisions, sometimes terrible ones, at other times good. Either way, men died. Far too many.

Going back to the start of the war, we look first at the South. In June 1861, the Confederate Army of Northern Virginia began as the Confederate Army of the Potomac. Adding forces from the Army of Shenandoah and forces from the District of Harper's Ferry, the Army of Northern Virginia became the main army of the Confederate South.

It was under the command of General E. Johnston that the Army of Northern Virginia fought in its first campaign in the First Battle of Manassas. Also called the Battle of Bull Run, this battle was a decisive victory, and Johnston was shown to be an excellent commander. The same could not be said for the other generals on the field.

Unfortunately, Johnston was injured during the Battle of Seven Pines which happened shortly thereafter, and command was then given to Major General Gustavus Smith, who held the command for all of two days before he suffered an apparent nervous breakdown and was replaced by General Robert E. Lee, who would then command for the remainder of the war. Under Lee, the Army of the Northern Virginia met the Iron Brigade at Antietam.

Let's back up a minute and talk about the North. In October of 1861, the Union Army commissioned the 3rd Brigade under Major General Irvin McDowell. This comprised the 2nd, 7th, and 6th Wisconsin Brigades and the 19th Indiana. A year later the 24th Michigan joined the brigade and found themselves severely tested at the second Battle of Bull Run. This brigade called themselves the Black Hats, but in subsequent battles, including Antietam, they distinguished themselves in battle and became widely known as the Iron Brigade.

This is where they came up against Lee for the first time. It wouldn't be the last.

While the Iron Brigade became known as some of the fiercest fighters in the Civil War, they weren't exactly on the winning side over the next few campaigns. While Antietam (Sept 17, 1862) was declared a Union victory, the losses were high. The Iron Brigade went next to Fredericksburg, where they were routed by Lee and his forces after a drawn-out campaign that lasted from Dec. 11th through the 15th. Later they would fight at Chancellorsville from April 30th through May 6th, 1863, where again the army would be routed and forced to retreat. By this point the Iron Brigade had been fighting together for more than two years, but under General Joseph Hooker, they just couldn't seem to win. As Robert K. Beecham, an infantryman from the 2nd Wisconsin later said, "The Chancellorsville Campaign pretty thoroughly demonstrated the fact the as a general in the field at the head of an army, General Joseph Hooker is no match for General Robert E. Lee."

After the battle at Chancellorsville, the Iron Brigade was camped at the Rappahannock River's northern bank at their winter quarters. The Union Army covered likely crossing points and protected the supply line but morale was low.

A member of the 7th Indiana who had missed the Battle of Chancellorsville said the Brigade was "in a comatose state." However not everyone agreed with this assessment, or at least not the cause of it. A member of the 102nd stated that,

"The talk of demoralization in the army is all false. The army is no more demoralized today then the day it first started out, although God knows is has had, through the blundering of inefficient commanders, and other causes too numerous to mention, plenty of reason to be."

General Hooker focused his energies on divining the movements of General Lee's forces. During the Battle at Chancellorsville, two of Lee's divisions had been notably absent. Given how badly outnumbered the Confederacy was, this seemed particularly suspicious. To gather intelligence, Hooker created The Bureau of Military Information and set Colonel George H. Sharpe at its head.

Sharpe was a highly educated man, fluent in several languages and a combat veteran. It was the responsibility of the Bureau to collect, analyze, and collate information from many diverse sources – from their own people, from deserters and prisoners from the other side, and from scouts to name a few. But because the Bureau was a new creation, Sharpe and his men often did not receive support from the Union army, and constantly had to fight to get the job done that they were created to do. If anything, the majority of Union command seemed suspicious of someone sent to gather intelligence, or were just plain not sure what they were supposed to do with him.

Be that as it may, Sharpe dug into his new job with gusto. Numbers were the goal at this point. Sharpe was still trying to figure out the Confederate strength and was creating a map of the opposing army's structure. The data they had was old and no longer viable, especially since Lee had completely reorganized the army in that spring of 1863. The lack of information suited Hooker just fine though. He had no desire for information to be found, as he'd been inflating the numbers of the enemy to explain why he kept losing battles. The last thing he wanted was an accurate head count.

Hooker was up to mischief in other ways. He'd begun a dangerous game with President Lincoln and Lincoln's chief military advisor, General Halleck. In an attempt to bypass the chain of command (because he was positive that Halleck was trying to undermine him and make him look bad – something that may not have been entirely inaccurate) he'd started reporting directly to Lincoln and bypassing Halleck altogether. When Lincoln called him on it, he said he didn't "expect justice at his [Halleck's] hands." Lincoln contacted both of them and basically told them to play nice.

Hooker wasn't listening. By mid-June he was disobeying orders, taking his own initiative, and trying to prove himself entirely on his own.

This wasn't a wise move. Lee had been expecting just that.

Chapter Two

Oh Brother, Where Art Thou?

"I wish I could get at those people over there."

—General Robert E. Lee

In the meantime, Lee was reorganizing his troops into three divisions from two, making them more flexible and lessening the total number of troops each of his generals had to command. It was this restructuring that was occupying Sharpe's men.

Lee's reorganization had its pitfalls though. Out of thirty-seven brigades, thirteen were entrusted to men without any kind of experience at this level of military leadership. Of the nine infantry divisions, three were handed to men who likewise did not have the experience to lead them. Also, with so much moving around, there was some confusion within the army too in regards to who to report to and how to work together. They needed time to become a cohesive fighting unit. They weren't going to be given that.

For the men, one of the Confederacy's soldiers remarked that he could stand on their "brest works [sic] and see the enemy on theirs."

Initially this was a relatively quiet time. One infantryman recorded listening to the sounds of a mockingbird. Another recounted how he and a few friends returned from drawing rations with nine unguarded hams that they'd felt the need to liberate. If the Union Army was dispirited, it did not carry through to the Confederacy. These men there were in high spirits.

But General Lee wasn't. In fact, he was rather frustrated. Lee sent a message to the Confederate President, Jefferson Davis, complaining that General Daniel Harvey Hill was refusing to send men currently set to defend North Carolina. He argued that there was no battlefront in North Carolina currently and General Hill had no need of so many men. In frustration, he said to the Confederate Secretary of War that Hill's promise to send men was little more than an "administrative smokescreen." Lee could no longer wait for promises from Davis for more men.

Lee needed to move.

Lee's own intelligence wasn't half bad either. He knew very well that Sharpe hadn't been able to get a reasonable count of his men, or track his movements. To him, it was time to take action. It was time to invade Union held lands – and aim for Washington itself. The trick was to sneak an entire army in under the nose of the enemy.

A division under General Ewell was to march toward Culpeper Courthouse, with General Longstreet's troops following closely thereafter, to draw Hooker away from Fredericksburg and equally away from his primary orders to guard Washington D.C. at all costs.

Lee was confident. He knew his enemy well. Hooker had behaved exactly as Lee had suspected that he would at Chancellorsville, and he was depending on Hooker now.

Lee moved his entire army to Culpeper, save for 20,000 men under the command of A.P. Hill, who now faced Hooker's 80,000 men. For Lee's plan to work, the Union observers would have to be fooled, but this was made more problematic by Sharpe's men who were now doing reconnaissance in hot air balloons.

But these balloons rarely went within bullet range. Regardless, there was something about being in a giant inflated object floating over the earth with gunfire erupting from all around. Typically the balloon operators would panic under fire and rapidly descend. A few snipers could keep them entirely at bay, and frequently did just that.

Lee also marched the men at night, and camped in heavy wooded areas during the day. This was a cold camp, without fires to cook by. Most of the men had no idea where they were going, but came away with a strong feeling of "something's up." Rumours abounded, some even accurate. The boys were eager to fight.

But despite all his precautions, not all the movements of the men went unnoticed. "Balloon reports from Bank's Ford two camps disappeared and several batteries in motion," stated a headquarters circular. Others reported a "line of dust" and another, "20 wagons moving northerly."

Suddenly, the quiet Union army stirred. Under a barrage of cannon fire, they sent skirmishers after the sharpshooters and infantry at a river crossing south of Fredricksburg and established a hold on the river's south side.

The problem was, this was exactly what Hooker had been ordered NOT to do.

General Lee spent June 6th observing the new position of Hooker's army. As it seemed that there were no forces to take advantage of the new ground gained, Lee ordered the march continued and sent word to Richmond that he too was leaving Fredericksburg. Once again, Lee had correctly estimated Hooker's strategies.

Lee reached Culpeper the next day and sent a message again to Richmond, in which he implied that his move was necessary to match the redeployment of the Union Army. He gave no implication that this was instead a staging ground for another incursion into the north.

In the meantime, Sharpe's men had finished their reorganized charts and tables of all the changes in Lee's army, noting that the two divisions had in fact become three, and men were dispersed to new camps following the change. General Hooker used this information to explain the disappearances of the enemy troops, assuming they had been absorbed into the new divisions, and that all the motion the balloons had reported could be attributed to that.

Sharpe too misread the data. He was convinced that Lee would plan a cavalry charge, and that Lee's infantry (which Sharpe believed was still at Fredericksburg) would fall back and reinforce the Confederate stronghold in Richmond, and then move on to the war in the West.

On June 7th, Hooker sent word to his cavalry commander, Major General Alfred Pleasanton, to cross the river and proceed with the entire cavalry to Culpeper.

The Union plan was to cross the river at Brandy Station and Kelly's Ford and to meet at Brandy Station to regroup and attack the Confederates at Culpeper. The military intelligence was somewhat misleading though, as the

Confederate cavalry was in Brandy Station. Thus half of the invading Union cavalry found itself engaged against the entire Southern cavalry.

However, the Confederacy, having no idea that an enemy attack was due, had had a "grand review" of pomp and grandeur in honour of their commander, Robert E. Lee, and were entirely unprepared.

Dispatching a letter to Hooker, Pleasanton noted that their plans had been compromised, but that he was continuing on. They overran a company at Beverly's Ford and halted near St. James Church. Here they met with a devastating counterattack, where the Union cavalry was held in check, unable to proceed.

The rest of the Union cavalry was delayed at Kelly's Ford until 9:00 a.m. Once across the river, they split their forces in two, one half going to Brandy Station and the other to Stevensburg. Jeb Stuart, in command of the Confederate cavalry, ordered some of his troops to Kelly's Ford, and rode to St. James to reinforce the battle there.

There were two roads to Kelly's Ford and Stuart's men took the one that the Union cavalry did not take. By noon, Stuart was receiving frantic dispatches that Union forces were already well to his rear. He sent regiments from St. James to meet the approaching forces from the south.

North and South met at Fleetwood Hill and for a few hours, mounted attack met mounted attack. The terrain of the hill led to several small skirmishes as riders shot, stabbed, and rammed each other, while riderless horses, some injured, some dying, screamed and ran in every direction.

The portion of the force that had headed to Stevensburg countermarched to reinforce the battle at Fleetwood. Though the Union was beginning to make gains, Pleasanton called a halt and retreated back across the river, confident that his orders had been carried out to "disperse and destroy the enemy."

But prisoners taken at Brandy Station confirmed the information Sharpe so badly needed. Lee had moved his troops, and the General was with them.

Chapter Three

Rumors of War

"I shall direct him to give you orders, and you to obey them."

—Abraham Lincoln

Reactions to the news was somewhat varied. Pennsylvania's citizens were warned that rebels were poised to invade. They were asked to swell the ranks of the militia but the response was lukewarm at best. The people were complacent, and no one really felt that Lee would dare to invade the North.

Hooker was anything but complacent though. He sent a message to Lincoln, asking permission to march on Richmond, again bypassing Halleck in the correspondence. Lincoln told him no in no uncertain terms. "Lee's army, and not Richmond, is your true objective."

Lincoln then showed Halleck everything that Hooker had said. Halleck wrote to second everything Lincoln had already said. Hooker then went on the defensive, telling them he was badly outnumbered (still with no proof of numbers to back himself up).

But by June 13th, Sharpe had proof of Lee's movements. Hooker felt it was time to advance. The problem was in knowing where the troops were exactly. Hooker's information was old.

Lee's orders were to clear the Shenandoah Valley for the sake of being able to move the Confederate Army into position to go after Washington. The troops finally engaged at Winchester June 13th through the 15th, a battle that went firmly into the hands of the Confederates. Morale increased in the invading army. Their capture of supplies and defeat of a Northern city held them in high spirits. The Union was stunned that they had lost.

Hooker was also getting into hot water. On June 16th he found the enemy at Harper's Ferry. A lengthy correspondence between himself and Halleck put Hooker into a corner where he proclaimed that as ordered (which he hadn't been) he would march to Harper's Ferry and engage the enemy there. Lincoln himself got involved and told him to sit down and shut up, as he hadn't been ordered anywhere. He also told Hooker to start listening to Halleck. The "or else" was understood in these lines,

To remove all misunderstanding, I now place you in strict military relation to General Halleck of a Commander of one of the armies to the General-in-Chief of all the armies. I have not intended differently, but as it seems to be differently understood, I shall direct him to give you orders, and you to obey them.

Skirmishes continued up and down the valley. Sharpe scrambled to keep up with the information, much to the frustration of all involved. He felt strongly that Lee would have to fight Hooker somewhere before moving on to Maryland or Pennsylvania. The question was where.

Hooker in the meantime was rumoured to have turned to strong drink. Lincoln was mediating between Hooker and Halleck. Public opinion regarding Hooker was fading fast.

In Gettysburg, there was talk of advancing armies. Every citizen was on the alert, and gossip exclusively turned to talk of troop movements. Tensions rose…and then fell as day after day passed and a certain strange normalcy to being surrounded ensued.

This would all soon change.

Chapter Four

Hooker's Last Stand

"I did my share in getting rid of Hooker, in whom I never had confidence."

—Brigadier General George Washington Cullum

On June 26th the 26th Pennsylvania Emergency Infantry marched through Gettysburg. These were boys newly enlisted, still learning the drills. The citizenry greeted them with a warm breakfast.

Just west of Gettysburg, a small Union force led by William Jennings had encountered a small road block. The Confederates couldn't resist the challenge and engaged. It wasn't long before the road block lay in tatters. The Confederate forces swept into the town, shouting and shooting their guns in an attempt to scare the residents. Instead several looked at the whole incident as entertainment, peering at the invaders though attic windows. It wasn't all fun and games though. The activity flushed out some Union soldiers from hiding. One, Private Sandoe, was shot and killed, becoming the first casualty in what was about to become a deadly battle.

This initial group of rebels were wild, taking what they wanted with little regard for the residents. This changed when Gordon brought his infantry into town. This new group of Confederates were more polite, even termed businesslike in their occupation. This was followed by the rest of the infantry led by Jubal Early. They demanded money and supplies. No one could pay the ransom though, and goods were in limited supply. Upon finding a railcar filled with rations, they took that instead. They spent the night and then moved out the next day.

Meanwhile Hooker was after more men. He went up against Halleck, demanding, and getting, more soldiers, claiming to be vastly outnumbered though Sharpe's information wasn't backing him up in the least. His goal was once again Harper's Ferry.

At this point communications broke down again, ending in a long back and forth that ended in Hooker asking to be relieved of command. To his surprise, this was very quickly accepted. General George Meade was appointed in his place only three days prior to the battle.

The entire matter of this animosity between Hooker and Halleck bears some examination by historians. The question is, how much of this was Hooker's desire to do what he wished, and to make excuses, and how much was Halleck trying to get in his way? There are arguments strong in favor of each man, though Halleck comes out as being more of the aggrieved hero of the piece. Had Hooker intended to resign, or had it been said in a fit of pique? Regardless, he was out, and now a brand new General would assume command on the threshold of what would be the turning point of the war.

Chapter Five

Everything Comes Together

"You are marching mighty proudly now, but you will come back faster than you went"

—Woman at roadside, to Confederate forces

The troops passing through Gettysburg on June 28, 1863 had no intention of staying. They were part of a patrol, so when the residents came out to cheer them as they marched down the main street of town, there was a certain amount of awkwardness. They weren't there to protect, only to pass through. The Union soldiers set up camp just outside of town, with every intention of moving on in a day or two.

The residents though felt safe and protected to have the army so close by. This would change quickly in the next few days.

On June 29th, Lee heard the news the Army of the Potomac had indeed crossed the river that bore its name. Lee didn't like it. It sounded as though the Union army was trying to come up behind him and cut his forces into pieces. He gave a change in orders – head toward Chambersburg.

The Confederacy was well-prepared though. In a bit of action that showed excellent foresight, one of Jeb Stuart's men pulled down the telegraph lines between Baltimore and Frederick. Communications between the Union lines and Washington would be delayed at the very least.

George Meade was moving his forces as well. The main objective had shifted to protection of Washington and Baltimore at all costs.

It seemed like everyone was in motion that day. Some of the Confederate troops near Cashtown were in desperate need of boots. When they heard that there were some to be had in Gettysburg they hit the road. While they set out to find footwear, they instead found the Union encampment just outside of town. As the old saying goes, "For want of a shoe, the kingdom was lost." For want of a shoe…how many lives would be lost?

Forgoing the boots entirely, they retreated to report back to command what they had found.

By this time, Lee had found out about the change in command for the Army of the Potomac. He expressed concern, feeling that Meade would rush in to take advantage of any mistake he made. Those under him began to worry as well. Lee's advantage up until now was a solid understanding of his opponent. Meade was an unknown element.

In the meantime, the troops around Gettysburg were reported to Brigadier General J. Johnston Pettigrew of the Confederate forces. General Heth ordered him to Gettysburg, with the warning that they might find some kind of militia in the town. They also told him that if the troops turned out to be regular army to not engage but to retreat. Pettigrew was about to carry out this command when he got word that there were considerable enemy troops around the city. General Heth told him to press on regardless. It was June 30th, and Pettigrew arrived at Gettysburg about ten in the morning.

Being cautious, Pettigrew set up where he could spy out the lay of the land. In the distance he heard drums and bugles. That was good enough for him. He ordered a return to camp by 11:00 a.m.

In the meantime, Meade was still learning the command system of the army he'd been placed in command of only two days earlier. While his cavalry spread out in several small skirmishes, Meade struggled to keep on top of things. He fouled up by sending marching orders for several divisions that completely were at odds with previous orders from General Reynolds. The men under him started to lose confidence. Somehow he still managed to pull them together. Later it would be said that in a matter of days he had turned the Union army into a cohesive fighting force. Right now that was difficult to see.

Pettigrew meanwhile reported to his division commander, Heth, about everything he'd seen in Gettysburg. While they didn't feel it was a full army, they did feel it was worth further investigation. Heth took the matter to A. P. Hill, who dismissed the idea that there were trained troops at Gettysburg at all despite Pettigrew pulling over one of his men to verify the story.

Heth didn't like how the conversation was going. Finally he offered to take troops up to Gettysburg in the morning to investigate the matter. Reluctantly, Hill agreed.

On the Union side of things Pleasanton ordered John Buford to take his men to Gettysburg no later than the night of June 30th. Upon arriving, Buford didn't like the setup the city offered. Finally he took a guess that enemy troops would come from the area of Cashtown. With that in mind, he put the majority of his troops along McPherson Ridge, Herr Ridge, and Seminary Ridge to the west and north of town, more than three miles from the town centre.

The stage was set.

Chapter Six

Day 1: July 1, 1863

"My God, you are not going to fire here, are you?"

—Farmer Lohr upon seeing artillery set up in his front yard

Brigadier General Buford had thought this out. He knew the forces were coming and had planned carefully as to which direction he felt they would come. He kept in mind his own reinforcements on the way, Union infantrymen who would then be able to occupy Cemetery Hill, Cemetery Ridge, and Culp's Hill.

General Meade had also been busy. He'd been trying to figure out the movements of Lee all day on the 30th. When a message finally reached him, it would be only hours before dawn on July 1. "Lee is falling back suddenly from the vicinity of Harrisburg." The forecast called for Chambersburg being the destination. This verified what Meade had been thinking, and he likely went to bed much relieved in his mind of what the next day would bring. Sadly, those cut telegraph lines would come back to haunt him. There had been a second message sent after the first, one that was waiting for a courier to get to him. The destination was Gettysburg after all.

On the first day of the battle, July 1, 1863, the two sides made contact. The armies of both North and South had spent the pre-dawn hours on reconnaissance, sometimes skirting troops so close it's a wonder that they didn't see each other. It was Marcellus E. Jones that, upon seeing the red Confederate flag, took careful aim and fired a single shot. The battle had indeed commenced.

It all happened quickly. What had seemed like a lot of stumbling around in the woods, and just missing each other on opposite roads, suddenly became a full-on engagement.

Lee's men, under the direction of General A. P. Hill, rushed Buford's men at McPherson's Ridge. Buford's men fought a delaying action, and General Oliver O. Howard and his men held Cemetery Hill, a point fixed by the General as being too important to lose due to its height. His concentration was here when he was told, "General Reynolds is dead, and you are the senior officer on the field." Shock gave way to resolve to hold until the rest of the Union army could arrive.

Another corps of Confederate soldiers under Richard Ewell arrived. While his previous orders had been to not engage, when he saw the battle had already commenced, he threw his troops into the action to attack the Union flank. "It was too late to avoid an engagement without abandoning the position that was already taken up," he later reported. "I determined to push the attack vigorously."

Also attempting to control the high ground, General Francis Barlow moved his Union troops to a knoll along the Harrisburg Road. In retrospect, this move has been called "foolish", "disastrous", and "unspeakable folly."

Colonel Von Amsberg, in command of the First Brigade, pushed three regiments forward beating back the Alabama sharpshooters. Confederate artillery—two batteries—arrived then and forced the three regiments back, forcing them to form a defensive line 200 yards short of meeting up with the rest of the Union army, essentially stranding 950 men in a separate skirmish.

Orders of troop movements became impossible because of the artillery. Barlow had not received new orders from his superior, who was concentrating on the artillery barrage. Barlow did however receive orders to "extend the line according to [his] best judgement".

The Second Brigade joined Barlow and awaited further orders, but Barlow's men and the new additions were tempting targets for the artillery. After a quick assessment, Barlow formed his line at Blocher's Knoll and Rock Creek. This decision took advantage of the terrain, but put Barlow's men 700 yards out of position and on the wrong side of the road.

As a side note, Barlow had nothing but contempt for the 2,477 men under him. As he ordered them into position, he told an officer to "shoot down stragglers." There's question as to whether he threw his men into the fight in order to make them toughen up in to true soldiers. He certainly never said.

In the meantime, the 2nd Cavalry Brigade, having seen the approach of the more Union soldiers backed out of the skirmish they were fighting, seeing the newcomers as relief. The Union batteries on Cemetery Hill, however had a problem—the poor quality of the ammunition caused several of their shots to fall short, thus placing the 2nd Cavalry under friendly fire. After three of their own horses had been hit by wayward bullets, the Cavalry pulled back even further—to the other side of the town and out of the fighting.

Up on Cemetery Ridge, the Iron Brigade pushed back and forth. They were described by observers as "magnificent" – and their fervor in battle is what held the heights that day against enemy attack. Let by Lieutenant Colonel Rufus Dawes, they seemed unstoppable. Even when Dawes' horse was shot out from under him, he sprang clear, giving a shout of, "I'm alright boys!" His men cheered, and threw themselves right back into the advance.

The two divisions of the Confederates, 2,800 men, converged on Barlow's men with perfect timing. 1,300 more Confederate troops stood by the ready in case they were needed.

Another Union brigade organized to come to aid Barlow's men, but would not arrive until after Barlow was in full retreat. It had taken only about 15 to 20 minutes of hard fighting for Blocher's Knoll to be overrun. Union forces broke and ran rather than surrender, not ready to call it a day just yet.

For the next two hours, Confederate troops pushed the Union line ever back. Progress was slow and uneven, but the South kept the initial momentum going.

Barlow, attempting to rally his men, was shot twice and left on the battlefield where he became a prisoner of the Confederacy.

Blocher's Knoll, now known as Barlow's Knoll, was a source of defeat and humiliation for the young general. Some contemporaries called Barlow's defeat a rout, and casualties were drastically high for the Union troops.

The Union was forced to retreat off of McPherson's Ridge as well, amidst a great deal of confusion. Among the last to leave was a color-bearer, who paused every now and then in his retreat to shake a fist at the Confederate forces. Finally, he too fell, victim of a Confederate bullet.

Losses on the first day of fighting were tremendous. Of the two divisions of Confederates, one lost 1,153 casualties out of 1,829 men, and the other lost 1,500 out of 7,000. In total numbers, of the 23,500 Union solders, approximately 9,000 (nearly 40%) were casualties. Of the Confederates' 28,300 men, approximately 6,000 lost their lives.

Lee arrived just as the Union were forced to retreat. He gave his junior the option to pursue or retire for the night, though he himself was still anxious to fight.

General Ewell, having just ridden through the troops, and receiving the compiled reports from those under him, considered the devastating losses. He looked at his tired troops. After a long pause, he declared that the first day of fighting had ended.

Chapter Seven

Day 2: July 2, 1863

"You are to hold this ground at all costs"

—Colonel Strong Vincent

At the close of day previous, the Union army had held a great deal of the high ground – Culp's Hill, Cemetery Hill, and Cemetery Ridge - that included a hill down at the end known as Little Round Top. This high ground would prove to be an advantage in the fighting, with the Confederates forced to attack uphill – both wearying and a severe tactical disadvantage. The mood was therefore hopeful.

So on this, the second day of the battle, General Meade arranged his men along Cemetery Hill. Two divisions under Major General Daniel E. Sickles would be anchored by Little Round Top. Sickles, having inspected the area he was to defend, noted that the terrain was barely higher than the flat areas around it. He sought to change his position to a peach orchard on a more prominent hill to the west.

Sickles sent out a reconnaissance force into the grove along Cemetery Ridge where it was repulsed by a greater number of Confederate troops.

Sickles occupied the grove and anchored his men to the Devil's Den, a boulder-strewn ridge south of town. This put his men at two thirds of a mile from the Southern Army.

It also left Little Round Top open, and vulnerable to attack.

Sickles had disobeyed orders. A former schoolteacher and college professor, Colonel Joshua Laurence Chamberlain brought his men, the 20th Maine, around to save it. As they scrambled into position and built fortifications there was a feeling of being too late. Already they were hearing the advancing troops, and that distinctive Rebel Yell.

It seemed only moments before the 15th Alabama regiment threw themselves up the hill. Again and again they were repulsed. The air was thick with smoke. Chamberlain himself was shot, but the bullet hit his sword, leaving him bruised but unbloodied.

Spread thin, but fighting fiercely with everything they had, the day advanced with chaos and a barely held line. "At times, I saw around me more of the enemy than of my own men," Chamberlain later recalled.

Robert E. Lee received word that the Union's left flank was "vulnerable" and elected to exploit this opportunity by sending Longstreet and his men against it. To arrive in a surprise attack, Longstreet would have to head south for more than three miles and then turn east. This needed to be done while avoiding detection. Longstreet would not be in position until late afternoon.

In the meantime, General Meade, hearing the sound of battle, found Sickles' men engaged with the enemy. Sickles' men were exposed and far in front of the line. To Meade it seemed that the position was indefensible, but it was too late to fall back to Cemetery Ridge. Longstreet was beginning to move in, so Meade, out of desperation. called in the troops he'd had in reserve to move in and reinforce the position. In the meantime, he pulled men from Culp's Hill to fill the position.

Longstreet began that afternoon with an artillery barrage against the peach orchard. He split his forces in two parts under Lafayette McLaws and John B. Hood, one to attack the Devil's Den and the other to attack the orchard. After fierce fighting with a great loss of life on both sides, the Union Army gave ground at Devil's Den and the Confederate Army took position of it.

But not of Little Round Top.

Five times the rebels broke through the lines. Five times the 20th Maine pushed them back. They were running out of ammunition when Chamberlain saw the Confederate army bracing for another attack. "Bayonets!" he shouted in what had to be one of the most heroic moments of the day. The Rebels were only 30 feet away.

With a roar they charged.

It was violent. It was bloody. In the end they held the hill at terrible cost. Chamberlain lost 10% of his men, but at day's end they still held the high ground.

The battle for the orchard continued. The reserve men arrived too late for the Confederate attack. The Southerners flanked the orchard and sent the Union Army into a retreat. Only the fall of darkness halted the Confederate advance.

Ewell in the meantime was attacking the Union right flank with artillery. Brigadier General George Green commanded a single brigade, as Meade had pulled many of his men to cover Cemetery Hill when Sickles was out of position. Green stretched his men over a large area, but several breastworks were left unmanned.

The Confederate army flanked Green and occupied the lower portions of Culp's Hill. Direct attacks against Green, however, proved to be fruitless. Reinforcement for Green's men arrived Cemetery Hill, but by the time help arrived, darkness had already fallen.

While the battle at Culp's Hill raged on, the Confederates attacked Cemetery Hill from the north. Two brigades defended the heights, but the Union Army had been shifting to cover open areas and developed a gap in the line at about the same time the Southerners attacked.

The Confederacy exploited this weakness and tore through the Union line. They were able to reach the artillery batteries before reinforcements could arrive.

As darkness fell on the battlefield, the Union Army held its position and the Confederacy had not gained any ground.

Chapter Eight

Day 3: July 3, 1863

"I have no division now."

—General George E. Pickett

General Lee wanted to end the battle at Gettysburg with a decisive victory, but the Union troops opened the morning with battery fire from Culp's Hill. When the barrage was finished, Lee sent Ewell and Johnson's troops to attack on three different attempts, but the entrenched Union soldiers rebuffed the attackers each time and the confederacy could not get a toe-hold on the hill. Given that the troops thought the whole thing was "suicidal" it's not surprising they couldn't take it.

Reinforcements called the day before had arrived the previous night, and the Union line was now virtually impenetrable. Lee planned an extensive barrage of cannon fire along the Union line, and a direct attack of 12,000 men down the enemy's center.

This was the second plan that day that looked like a suicide move. Longstreet protested. It seemed like it would be a better plan to dig in and wait for Meade to attack them. Lee responded by pointing across the fields and saying, "The enemy is there, General Longstreet, and I am going to strike him."

Longstreet set the works in motion, choosing General George Pickett, General Isaac R. Trimble, and Brigadier

General James Pettigrew. Pickett was enthusiastic, feeling that his men would finally be able to prove themselves. Pettigrew's men were in bad shape already, something Lee didn't know at the time.

At 1:00pm Lee's one hundred forty cannon unleashed their fire along the opposite line, concentrating on the Union cannons. If they would take out the cannon, then the way would be clear for Pickett and his men. Also, injuring as many Union men as possible prior the charge would swing the odds in their favor.

The firefight lasted for two hours, filling the field with smoke, and shaking the ground underfoot. Suddenly the Union stopped firing. It looked like they were out of ammunition. The Confederacy likewise ceased firing.

There was a moment of hesitation. Pickett was waiting for the command. Longstreet looked at the waiting troops and, very aware that he might be sending these boys to their deaths, finally nodded.

The men stepped forward. 13,000 men in parade formation – the first row nearly a mile wide. Row following row. Said a Union officer later, "[They moved] as with one soul, in perfect order…magnificent, grim, irresistible."

It had been a trap.

Meade had guessed what was coming next, proving that war was really a matter of out-Generaling the other guy. They opened fire with everything they had. Men fell by the dozens. Yet Pickett never stopped urging them on. Holes in the line were filled with more men…and more men. The losses were devastating. It looked like they would make it over the wall.

A handful managed to do it. They overwhelmed their targets and captured several Union cannons. They'd managed to cross 1,400 feet of open, unprotected ground.

When air cleared and the dirt settled, the Confederates discovered they'd created no significant damage to the Union batteries – in fact the Union had only lost a few infantrymen. Most of the Rebel fire had overshot their intended targets. They had sent their men into hell unknowing.

Pettigrew's men followed the charge to the left of Pickett. He continued on foot, after his horse was shot out from under him, and then was wounded himself as he neared the wall. There he held his position and encouraged the troops until it became apparent that the whole thing was a terrible failure.

Trimble followed Pettigrew in, but was wounded early on. He called to his men to retreat.

This whole affair came to be known as Pickett's Charge, due to the enthusiasm and heroism of the advance. It's a sad footnote to history that no one acknowledges the part that Trimble or Pettigrew played, when in fact they'd been every bit as courageous, perhaps even more so given the poor state their troops were in.

Led by General Lewis A. Armistead, a group of about 300 Virginians made it over the wall. Their position wasn't good however. The wedge formation that had carried them to the center of the enemy front proved to be a mistake when the army flanked the attackers and were able to fire into them with devastating results.

In the end, their numbers alone couldn't do the job. No reinforcements came to save them, and the Union fire was heavy. The Confederates were forced to withdraw without having gained any ground at all.

Nearly 5,600 men, more than 50% of the entire attacking force, were killed or wounded in the assault. Losses to the Union soldiers are estimated to be about 1,500.

Lee had sent General Stuart with four brigades of cavalry around the Union's right flank, supposed to take advantage of any victory by the infantry. About three miles east of Gettysburg, Stuart ran into two brigades of Union troops commanded by General McGregg.

Resulting attack and counter-attack would prove to be the bloodiest cavalry battle of the war, with great losses of men and horse. Interestingly enough the majority of the battle had been fought with cavalry saber, rather than firearm, and had degenerated into hand to hand combat on foot. The battle between cavalry would end in a draw, with McGregg holding his ground and Stuart gaining nothing at all.

At the end of it all, Lee, not realizing yet the full extent of his defeat, turned to Pickett and started to give him the order to regroup and fight again. Pickett stared at him in disbelief. "General. I have no division now."

As the reports came in, Lee realized the full extent of what had happened. The war they'd been fighting on the offensive was now a thing of the past. To continue to fight would be a defensive move. It was time to retreat and protect his army, or what was left of it.

Meade was coming to similar realizations. At the end of the day he tested his men, and found them wanting.

I went immediately to the extreme left of my line, with the determination of advancing the left and making an assault upon the enemy's lines. So soon as I arrived at the left, I gave the necessary orders for the pickets and skirmishers in front to be thrown forward to feel the enemy, and for all preparation to be made for the assault. The great length of the line, and the time required to carry these orders out to the front, and the movement subsequently made, before the report given to me of the condition of the forces in the front and left, caused it to be so late in the evening as to induce me to abandon the assault which I had contemplated.

Later Meade would be criticized for this decision, as it would be thought he had missed the opportunity to destroy Lee's army once and for all.

Regardless, for better or for worse, the battle was finally over.

Chapter Nine

Aftermath

"It has been a sad, sad day for us"

—General Robert E. Lee

Throughout the course of the conflict, curious citizens had wandered out to watch. Most of them had been turned back, sometimes angrily, by soldiers who feared for the safety of the impetuous souls that they felt they couldn't protect on the battlefield.

Now it was Lee who stood and stared out over the field, perhaps trying to settle in his own mind as to what had just happened.

Heavy rains made the retreat difficult. Meade followed Lee and his men as they pulled out of Virginia, trailing half-heartedly behind, with no one eager to get involved in a fight again. The rain-swollen Potomac made crossing difficult. In the end Lee and the Army of Northern Virginia made it back home, never to cross into Union territory again

For the people of Gettysburg the horror was only just beginning. They had already been tending the wounded in their barns and homes since the first shot was fired and the first man injured. Now came the clean-up, a truly disgusting job. There were thousands of bodies that had accumulated under the blisteringly hot summer sun, followed by heavy rain and mud. These bodies were swollen and grotesque. The ground grew so saturated that it was described that there were puddles of blood.

Add to this the horses, thousands of them as well, lying dead or screaming to be put out of their misery.

One can only imagine the repugnance in having to deal with all of this. One young girl described in her diary how repulsed she was by the injured, but after three days she was tending them. There came a new normalcy where people were called upon to do the difficult things. To burn the horses until the sky was filled with the stench of it, to the point where people were becoming sick. To bury not just the dead soldiers, but to deal with the fact that these boys were someone's son or husband. To deal with the fact that some of them were their own husbands and sons.

But they were also burying things unspeakable – veritable mountains of amputated limbs that piled high outside of windows where hasty operations were being performed.

And yet people still kept dying. The injured succumbed to disease and gangrene. Yet somehow life had to go on.

It's amazing to note that only one civilian died in all of this. One young girl, Ginnie Wade, who was making bread in her kitchen, was felled by a stray bullet and died.

As for the soldiers, between 45,000 and 52,000 men were either dead, injured, captured or missing. The Union forces alone numbered just a bit over 23,000, with 3,155 dead on the field. The Confederacy is much harder to estimate and there's some debate as to that number, hence the range given here.

As a side note, the Iron Brigade (remember them?) suffered the most casualties of any brigade that fought at

Gettysburg. Losing 1,153 out of 1,885 men, this was 61% of their force.

This doesn't begin to account for property damage. Many buildings had been shelled. Livestock and supplies had been taken. The people of Gettysburg suffered greatly, and would for some time afterwards.

For many, life would never be the same.

Chapter Ten

This Hallowed Ground

"His face was wondrous to look upon."

—Albertus McCreary, upon observing Lincoln giving the Gettysburg Address

In October of 1863, a massive effort was underway to rebury the Union dead at Gettysburg. The Committee for the Consecration of the National Cemetery at Gettysburg sought to make the site a national monument.

President Lincoln was invited to, after the speeches, "formally set apart these grounds to their sacred use by a few appropriate remarks."

Lincoln arrived, his face very white, and even described as "haggard." He was later diagnosed with a mild case of smallpox. At the time of the ceremony he was dizzy and feeling ill, and had even remarked on it on the trip to Gettysburg.

The ceremony itself began with a marching band and the key speaker, Edward Everett. Everett was a pastor, a noted orator, and served in the Senate and in the House of Representatives. His was to be the "Gettysburg Address."

Everett's speech lasted two hours (a common length for the time), spoken before a crowd of about 15,000 people.

Lincoln's speech, however took a mere two minutes and in that short time summed up the war, its origins, and the hope of a nation.

Common lore says that Lincoln wrote the speech on the train on the way in. This might not be exactly true, and in fact some argue that it's more likely that he'd spent time writing it beforehand, and took time on the train to perhaps revise and proofread his remarks. The fact that it wasn't dashed off in a few minutes, makes it that much more valuable, as one can then realize the thought that has gone into every word and the careful meaning he put to each. Lincoln had a reputation for putting a great deal of store by choosing his words carefully, as can be seen in much of his correspondence - his communications with Hooker prior to Gettysburg case in point.

In the speech itself, Lincoln closes with the phrase "Government of the people, by the people, for the people…" The origin of this phrase may be traced to several sources, the first to one of the first English translations of the Bible in 1384. When John Wycliffe dedicated the work he stated in part, "This Bible is for the government of the people, for the people, and by the people." Or the phrase may simply have been taken from an abolitionist minister from Massachusetts whom Lincoln had read. Lincoln had marked a phrase in one of his sermons, which read, "Democracy is direct self-government, over all the people, for the people, and by the people."

Regardless of its origins, the speech so hastily crafted by a man so ill that he was described by some witnesses as "ghastly" was reprinted in the papers and became both a rallying cry, and a balm for the enormous amount of life lost.

Everett's 13,600+ word speech is most often forgotten today as the speaker himself is. Despite its eloquence, the sentiment of the two-hour speech and Lincoln's short acceptance at the site of the battle are saying the very much the same thing: that freedom comes with a dreadful price, those who defend that peace at the expense of their lives have paid that price, and that sacrifice sanctified the very ground where they had died, transforming it into hallowed ground.

During the time of this dedication, the war was not going well for the Union. Despite the fact there were no further attempts to enter the north by Lee, battles were going against the Union. The speech was reprinted in every paper in the country, unifying the war-weary Union and putting the Civil War into a new perspective: an over-arching history of the young republic.

Four score and seven years ago, our fathers brought forth on this continent a new nation, conceived in liberty, and dedicated to the proposition that all men are created equal.

Now we are engaged in a great civil war, testing whether that nation, or any nation so conceived and so dedicated, can long endure. We are met on a great battlefield of that war. We have come to dedicate a portion of that field as a final resting place for those who here gave their lives that the nation might live. It is altogether fitting and proper that we should do this.

But, in a larger sense, we cannot dedicate, we cannot consecrate, we cannot hallow this ground. The brave men, living and dead, who struggled here, have consecrated it, far above our poor power to add or detract. The world will little note, nor long remember what we say here, but it can never forget what they did here. It is for us the living, rather, to be dedicated here to the unfinished work which they who fought here have thus far so nobly advanced. It is rather for us to be here dedicated to the great task remaining before us – that from these honored dead we take increased devotion to that cause for which they gave the last full measure of devotion – that we here highly resolve that these dead shall not have died in vain – that this nation, under God, shall have a new birth of freedom – and that government of the people, by the people for the people, shall not perish from the earth.

Conclusion

The initial reaction to the Battle of Gettysburg among the Union was one of great happiness. This was a decisive victory that had saved their capital, and indeed had turned back the Confederates from a northern invasion overall. But as time went by, that feeling began to change.

Questions were asked. Why hadn't Meade finished the job? Why did there have to be such a great loss of life? A certain unhappiness settled in at the thought that the Civil War could go on for years yet, meaning more loss of property and more loss of life.

In the South the defeat was demoralizing. More than that, people were angry. Why had Lee lost when he had such a glorious army? It seemed as though there had been some mismanagement somewhere, and people wanted to place blame. Lee himself offered his resignation to Jefferson Davis on August 8, 1863. Davis refused it.

The loss of life was devastating. In three days, so much blood had been spilled. There were a lot of questions as to why, on both sides of the conflict.

Those who fought there took home more than battle scars. Haunted by their ordeal and by the decisions made, or not made as the case might be, there were a lot of questions. The semi-organized chaos of the battlefield had not been free of personalities, of people looking to build their own fame, or in some cases to save their own hides. Some people had behaved brilliantly, heroically even. Others, not so much. No one who was there and survived came away unscathed.

Overall the question arises, as it does to anyone who studies history – what is the significance of the battle? What have we learned from all of this?

The main importance is the fact that this was indeed a turning point for the war. This victory was decisive for the Union army, something that had been lacking. Also, Lee's plans to invade the north had come to a crashing halt. Never again would he get that far.

Some point out that Lee also lost about a third of his army, something that crippled him for quite some time afterwards. The effect on the morale of both North and South was significant, as even despite frustrations in regards to General Meade's lack of follow-through, there was still a strong sense of having come away a "winner."

Was there, as Lincoln said, a "new birth of freedom for the nation" that came out of this horrendous battle? Perhaps so, as this battle, more than any, acted as a unifying force to the American people, letting those in the Union know with no shadow of doubt that there was reason to fight this war. Prior to this moment there had still been many sympathizers, especially of the "live and let live" variety. Here now was ample proof that the South wasn't about to let anyone live in a way that wasn't compatible with their own belief system. Indeed if the South were willing to invade and kill Northerners on their own ground, then the war became a way of protecting their own homes, their own families.

And thus there was reason to fight after all.

It is said that in the long run, the battle served to unify again, but in a rather different way. Fifty years after the Battle of Gettysburg, on June 2th through July 6th, veterans from both sides of the conflict returned to Gettysburg. About 25,000 men showed up on the first day returned to camp, including the only surviving command officer, General Dan Sickles, to share stories and shake hands, finally laying to rest the animosity that had plagued the North and the South in the years after the war. By the peak of the celebration, there were more than 50,000 veterans in attendance, as well as several people who had lived in Gettysburg at the time of the battle.

Another such reunion was attempted at the 75th anniversary. Twenty-five veterans showed up for that event, an amazing number, given the years passed since the battle.

The question remains – could this have been done better? Could the war have turned around and the nation preserved some other way? It's hard to say. Had Lee succeeded, there's no telling what would have happened to the Union. Had Meade demolished the army at Gettysburg would the war have been over? These questions are hard ones that benefit, of course, from the gift of hindsight.

Regardless, the outcome was what it was, and Gettysburg changed the entire course of the Civil War from that point on. This alone makes it significant, and entirely worthy of study.

Printed in Great Britain
by Amazon

22101389R00030